LET'S BAKE A
CAKE

WRITTEN & ILLUSTRATED BY
RUTH WALTON

SEA-TO-SEA
Mankato Collingwood London

Every year, for my birthday, I go to my Grandma's house and we make a cake.

This year we made a chocolate cake.

What is your favorite kind of cake?

Grandma has her own recipe for chocolate cake.
You can find it on pages 26–27.

What do you think the cake is made of?

Sugar is the first **ingredient** in Grandma's recipe. It can be made from two different plants, but they are both made into sugar in nearly the same way.

This is **sugar beet**. The big **root** is made into sugar.

Root

Growing Sugar Beets
Sugar beets grow well in North America, northern Europe, and Russia. Farmers have fed sugar beets to their animals for a long time. Then, about 200 years ago, people began to make sugar from sugar beets.

This bulldozer is moving sugar beets from a big pile.

6

This is **sugar cane**. It is a type of grass that can grow up to 20 feet (6 m) tall! It likes to grow in **tropical** places.

Growing Sugar Cane

*The farmer has to wait patiently for the sugar cane to grow tall. Then he cuts the canes, ready to sell them to the factory where they will be made into sugar. Often the farmer isn't paid very much money and finds it hard to make a living. If we buy **fair trade** sugar, we can be sure the farmer has been paid fairly for his hard work.*

This farmer is cutting his sugar cane by hand.

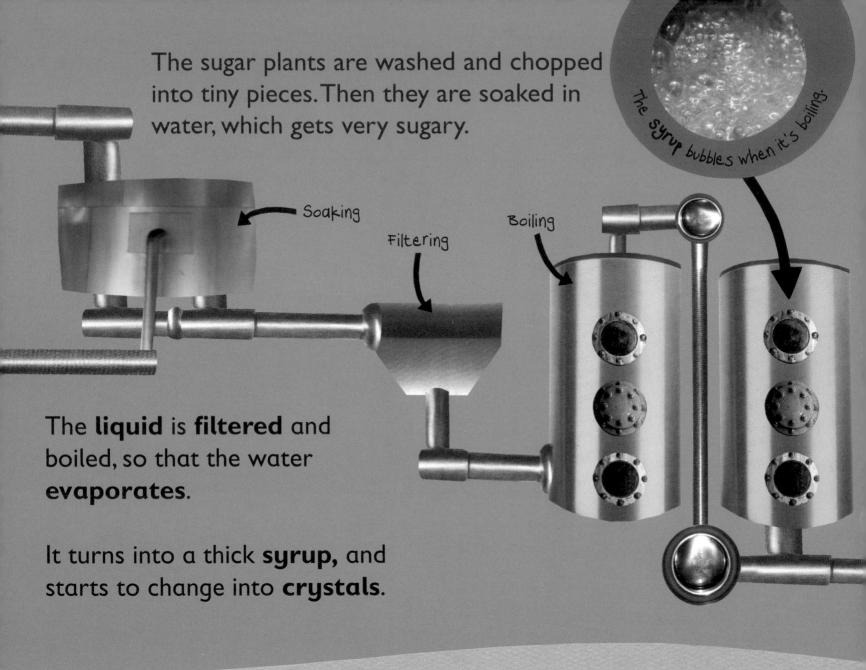

The sugar plants are washed and chopped into tiny pieces. Then they are soaked in water, which gets very sugary.

The syrup bubbles when it's boiling.

Soaking

Filtering

Boiling

The **liquid** is **filtered** and boiled, so that the water **evaporates**.

It turns into a thick **syrup,** and starts to change into **crystals**.

Which of these foods are made with sugar?

Cookies

Soft drinks

COLA

BEANS

Baked beans

The syrup is dried out in a machine called a **centrifuge**.

The sugar is ready to eat.

It is put into packages and taken to stores to be sold.

Spinning

The centrifuge is a bit like a giant spin drier!

Crystals

SUGAR

Chocolate

candy

ketchup

There is sugar in all of these foods, even the ketchup and baked beans!

9

Grandma's cake has lots of **butter** in it.
Butter is made from milk.

Cows make milk for their babies to drink.
A baby cow is called a calf.

Where Do Cows Live?

*In the countryside, you can see cows eating grass in the fields. During the winter, farmers keep the cows indoors in cowsheds. They feed them dried food, **hay**, and **silage.***

After the calves are taken away, the cows can be milked by people. We use the milk to drink and make **dairy** foods.

Female calves are raised to make milk. Some male calves are raised for meat, but others are **slaughtered** at birth.

The cow's **udder**, is where the milk comes from.

Do you know how milk is made into butter?

Most cows are milked twice a day, using electric pumps.

Every day, each cow can make about 8 gallons of milk.

The pumps are put onto the cow's udder...

The milk is **pasteurized**, and the fat is skimmed from the top. The fat from milk is called cream.

...and the milk travels through many pipes.

The cream is turned into butter by spinning it around using a churn.

Inside the churn, the cream separates into butter and **buttermilk**. Salt is often added, and the butter is **pressed**, to get rid of the water.

Before pressing...

...and after pressing.

The butter is wrapped, ready to be sold.

Now the butter is ready to be eaten!

Ice cream

Yogurt

Cheese

Cream

Chocolate drink

All of these things are made from milk!

Grandma's cake has three eggs in it. They help to **bind** the other ingredients together, because eggs go hard when you cook them.

All birds lay eggs, but people usually eat eggs laid by chickens. Female chickens are called hens.

The chickens eat a mixture of **grains**, with added vitamins, from special feeders that look like giant hats!

Do You Know Where Your Eggs Come From?

A lot of chickens are kept in tiny cages, or inside dark barns for their entire life. Imagine how you would feel if you were never allowed outside to play.

*If your egg carton says **free range** or **organic** on it, the chickens have been allowed to go outside for some fresh air and exercise.*

The hens lay eggs inside the henhouse or barn.

Every morning the eggs are gathered
and checked, ready to be sold.

The eggs roll onto racks under the hens' perches.

Eggs can be cooked in many different ways.

How do you like to eat your eggs?

One of the main ingredients in Grandma's chocolate cake is **flour**.

Flour is made from the grains of **wheat**, which is a type of grass. Most wheat is grown in North America, Europe, and Asia.

After the wheat is planted, the green shoots start to grow.

When Was Wheat First Grown?

People first grew wheat to eat around 10,000 years ago. They used stones called **querns** *to grind the grains into flour. In ancient times, people grew lots of different kinds of grain, but now farmers usually grow* **durum wheat**. *Look for foods made from other types of grain, such as spelt and rye.*

In summer, the sunshine turns the wheat a golden color, which means it is ready to **harvest**.

Farmers harvest wheat using a machine called a combine harvester, which separates the grains from the stalks.

Here is the combine harvester at work!

The wheat grains are taken to a **mill** to be made into flour. At the mill, the wheat grains are crushed by steel rollers, which is called milling.

Here are the grains falling into the rollers.

A Wheat Grain

The white part is called the endosperm.

This part is called the germ.

The brown part is called the bran.

The milled wheat is **sifted** to remove the bran. Whole-wheat flour has some bran left in it.

Bran

White flour

White flour has no bran in it. Self-rising flour has **baking powder** added to it.

FLOUR

The flour is put into packages.

Grandma uses white self-rising flour to make the chocolate cake.

All of these different foods are made from wheat.

Bread

Cookies

Pasta

Pastry for pies

Cereals

Noodles

When was the last time you ate some wheat?

19

This is a cacao tree, which is where **cocoa** comes from. Grandma uses cocoa to give her cake a chocolate flavor. Cacao trees grow in tropical forests in places like West Africa and South America.

Pod

Flower

The flowers and pods grow straight from the tree trunk.

If You Love Chocolate...
Then look after the cocoa farmers! Cacao trees often grow in countries where it is hard for farmers to earn enough money. Look for the fair trade symbol on chocolate and cocoa powder—it means farmers have been paid a good price for all their hard work, so that we can enjoy eating chocolate cake.

Cocoa flower

Cacao trees have tiny flowers. The flowers grow into pods, with **cocoa beans** inside.

Farmers pick the pods and split them open. Next, the cocoa beans are **fermented** and left to dry in the sunshine.

Cocoa pods

Cocoa beans

At a big factory, the beans are **roasted** and pressed to separate the **cocoa butter** from the pressed cocoa.

The pressed cocoa is ground up into powder, ready to be made into cakes or chocolate!

Cocoa powder

What is your favorite kind of chocolate?

When we have finished mixing the ingredients, we pour the batter into a cake pan and Grandma puts it into the oven.

Inside the oven, it's very hot. The heat makes moisture evaporate and the cake batter rises and becomes firm.

FLOUR

Confectioners' SUGAR

Sea Salt

Black Pepper

BEANS

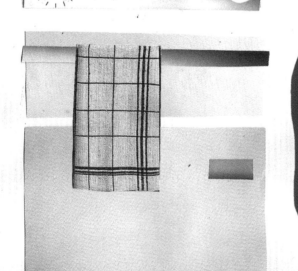

What Makes the Cake Rise?

The baking powder in the self-rising flour reacts with the cake batter to make tiny bubbles of **carbon dioxide**. *These get trapped inside the cake and help to make it rise up while it's baking!*

BAKING POWDER

While the cake is baking, we make frosting to spread on the top. When the cake is ready, Grandma takes it out of the oven.

Now the cake needs to cool so we tidy up. When the cake is cold enough, we spread the frosting all over the top. The cake is ready!

What kind of cake would you like to bake?

Where does it all come from?

 Wheat

 Sugar beet

 Sugar cane

 Cocoa

Which ingredient grows closest to where you live?

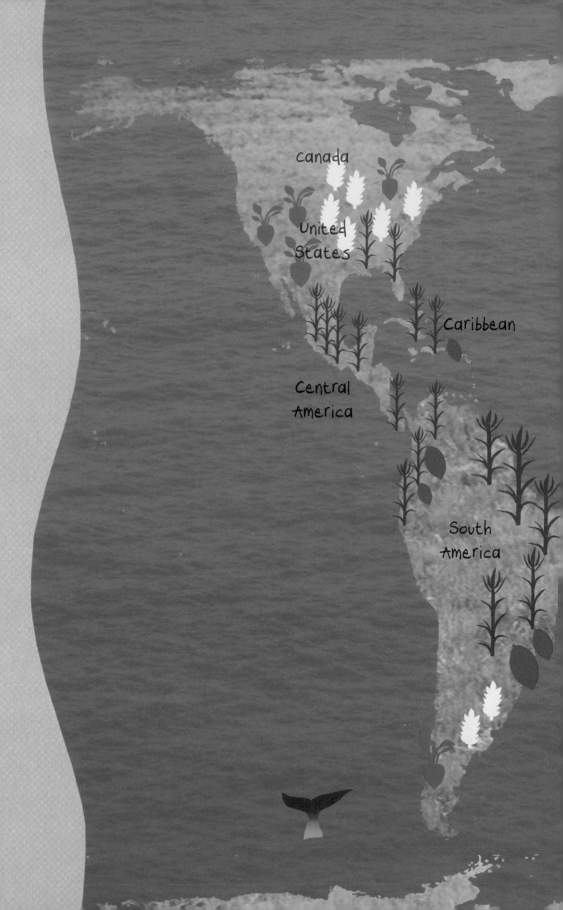

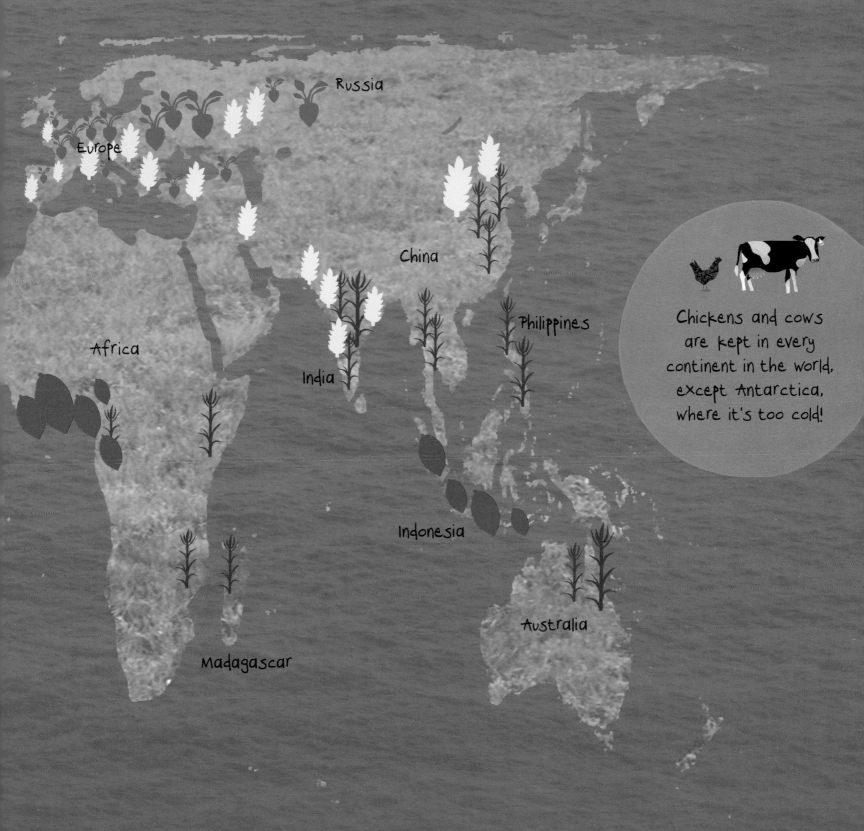

Russia

Europe

China

Philippines

Africa

India

Indonesia

Madagascar

Australia

Chickens and cows
are kept in every
continent in the world,
except Antarctica,
where it's too cold!

Antarctica

Make Your Own Chocolate Cake!

You will need about two hours and a grown-up to help you.

Start by finding all of these things in the kitchen:

For the cake:
¾ cup (175 g) butter
1½ cups (300 g) sugar
3 eggs

heaped ¾ cup (100 g)
self-rising flour
¾ cup (90 g) cocoa

For the icing:
¼ cup (50 g) butter
1 scant cup
confectioners' sugar
½ cup cocoa powder

Ask a grown-up to preheat the oven to 400°F (200°C) for you. Place the correct amount of sugar and then the butter in a measuring cup and add them to a big mixing bowl. Beat them together with a wooden spoon until pale yellow and creamy.

Break the eggs carefully into the bowl and mix them in too. Sift the flour and cocoa into the bowl through the sieve little by little. Continue to stir the batter until all the lumps are gone.

Grease an 8-inch (20-cm) cake pan by smearing a small amount of butter all around the inside. Don't miss any spots. Pour the batter in. **Ask a grown-up to put it in the oven** and then, after about 45 minutes, **take it out for you**.

To make the frosting, sift the confectioners' sugar and cocoa into a small bowl. Add the butter and mix it in well. If it's too dry, mix in a tablespoon of cold water, a few drops at a time. When the cake is cool, spread the frosting on top with a spatula.

Glossary

Baking powder a mixture of baking soda and cream of tartar used to help baked foods rise

Bind join together

Bran the tough outer part of a wheat grain

Butter the churned fat from milk

Buttermilk leftover liquid from making butter

Carbon dioxide a type of natural gas

Centrifuge a machine used for drying sugar

Cocoa brown powder made from cocoa beans

Cocoa beans seeds of the cacao tree, which grow inside cocoa pods

Cocoa butter fat from cocoa beans, used in cooking and cosmetics

Confectioners' sugar finely ground sugar, used for making frosting

Crystal a tiny piece of solid sugar

Dairy foods made from milk, and also the name for the place where they are made

Durum wheat the most commonly grown wheat

Endosperm part of a wheat grain

Evaporate turn from liquid into gas

Fair trade goods bought from farmers at a fair price

Fermented the process of breaking down a substance using heat or yeast

Filtered the process of separating solids from liquids

Flour powder made from ground wheat grains

Free range free-range farm animals must be able to spend at least part of each day outside

Germ part of a wheat grain

Grain dry, seedlike fruit produced by cereal crops

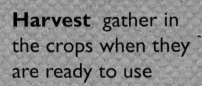

Harvest gather in the crops when they are ready to use

Hay grass that has been cut, dried, and stored for use as animal feed

Ingredient a substance that forms part of a mixture

Liquid a runny material, not a solid or gas

Mill the place where wheat is ground into flour, or the process of grinding it

Organic grown without using chemicals

Pasteurization process using heat to kill germs in food products

Perch somewhere a bird sits

Pressed squashed

Quern stone used to grind flour in the past

Roast cook with dry heat, usually in an oven

Root part of a plant below ground

Sift to separate by passing through a sifter to take out larger pieces

Silage animal feed that is made from green crops that can be stored for a long time

Slaughtered killed

Sugar sweet crystals made from sugar beets or sugar canes

Sugar beet plant with a large root used to make sugar

Sugar cane giant grass used to make sugar

Syrup a thick, sticky liquid

Tropical relating to or situated in the tropics (the region on either side of the equator)

Udder the part of a cow that makes milk

Wheat any of several cereal grains that can be made into flour

Index

This edition first published in 2013 by
Sea-to-Sea Publications
Distributed by Black Rabbit Books
P.O. Box 3263, Mankato, Minnesota 56002

Text and illustrations copyright
© Ruth Walton 2009, 2013

Printed in the United States of
America, North Mankato, MN.

9 8 7 6 5 4 3 2

Published by arrangement with the
Watts Publishing Group Ltd., London.

Library of Congress Cataloging-in-Publication Data

Walton, Ruth
  Let's bake a cake / written & illustrated by Ruth
Walton. -- 1st ed.
      p. cm. -- (Let's find out)
  Includes index.
  Summary: "Discusses where the ingredients for
making a chocolate cake come from, including the
plant or animal origins of sugar, butter, flour, eggs, and
cocoa. Includes recipe for chocolate cake"--Provided
by publisher.
  ISBN 978-1-59771-386-3 (alk. paper)
  1. Cake--Juvenile literature. 2. Baking--Juvenile
literature. 3. Chocolate desserts--Juvenile literature.
I. Title.
  TX771.W296 2013
  641.86'53--dc23

2011052692

Series Editor: Sarah Peutrill
Art Director: Jonathan Hair
Photographs: Ruth Walton, unless
otherwise credited

Picture credits: I Stock Photo:
8 (Lisa McDonald), 12 (Monica Perkins).
Shutterstock: 6 (Sascha Burkard), 7 (Hywit Dimyadi),
12 (Mark Yuill), 21tr (Dr. Morley Read).

*Every attempt has been made to clear copyright.
Should there be any inadvertent omission please
apply to the publisher for rectification.*

RD/6000006415/001

May 2012